DESTROY THE MASK

A Woman's Guide to Unlock Her True Self, Live Out Her Purpose, and Leave a Legacy of Power

ERIN FAITH KABBA

ISBN: 979-8-218-27677-5

Cover/Interior Design: Jean R. Wright and Anna Zubrytska
Editors: Miriam Arvinger and Iulia M.

For more information visit:
www.theoyacollective.com

Because of the dynamic nature of the internet, any web addresses or links contained in this book may have changed since publication and may no longer be valid. The views expressed in this work are solely those of the author and do not necessarily reflect the views of the publisher, and the publisher disclaims any responsibility for them.

Printed in the United States of America

To my daughter, you are a true light. May you live life to its fullest potential and do what you were created to do. I love you.

TABLE OF CONTENTS

INTRODUCTION

Welcome to *Destroy the Mask: A Woman's Guide to Unlock Her True Self, Live in Her Purpose, and Leave a Legacy of Power*, and thank you for purchasing this book. I hope that after reading this, you will be inspired to live life as who you were meant to be, have the audacity to pursue your purpose, and make a powerful impact on the world.

We were all born on purpose, with purpose. Our families, environment, beliefs, and habits have caused us to develop masks that hide our authentic selves. Some of us have been wearing a mask all our lives and have not been able to authentically show up due to things like societal expectations, harmful religious conditioning, systemic racism, misogyny, and the list goes on. For example, you may want to seek out certain career paths, but because you are a woman or a mother, you are discouraged from pursuing them. Perhaps you have different viewpoints and want to research and explore other ways of being or living, but you have been raised with the belief that adhering to the teachings of a specific religious denomination is the only path to follow.

You may be smiling on the outside because you have been playing the part and doing all the "right things," but deep down inside, you feel your true essence being choked out. Deep down you have desires, passions, and callings, but have been afraid to entertain the possibility of doing them because they do not align with the mask you are wearing. You have been doing all the things that align with the character you have been taught to portray, but it feels empty and inauthentic. There is a fire welling inside of you ready to come out, but fear, uncertainty, and shame keep it locked inside. I have been there. I know what you are going through.

All my life I wore a mask and played a character that did not align with who I was created to be. Religious conditioning, shame, systemic racism, and cultural norms caused me to not live as my authentic self and do things that were contrary to my passions or desires. I wrote this book to let you know that you CAN remove the mask and live as the woman you were designed to be.

One day, I found myself tired of doing things and following beliefs that did not serve me. I had passions and dreams I ignored due to fear and shame. I believed in God but was not sure about what I was told by others to believe about God. I knew I wanted to take big steps and follow certain career and life paths, but I knew that it went against the traditional trajectory of the path I was on. However, I was ready to go on a journey less traveled and take the steps to remove the mask and start living according to who I was created to be.

The first thing I did was deconstruct my faith and beliefs. My religion played a big part in forming my identity. I started to take inventory of what I believed, what my core values were, and what I wanted to do in life. I wanted to make a significant impact, but first I needed to get clear on who I was and what I was really supposed to do.

Through this reflection, I was able to achieve many of the desires and dreams that had been brewing in my soul for years. I got to know God on a deeper level without the barriers of harmful religious beliefs, and I decolonized my mind and saw myself as worthy. I destroyed limiting beliefs and tapped into the power I always had. I started a new career, established a new home, received the love my soul needed at the time, and started giving my child access to a life that I wanted her to have. I started a business, traveled, became a citizen of another country, and began to make an international impact. I was able to manifest and do all of this within two years. And you can do it too when you decide to remove the mask and have the courage to be led by the Divine. When you boldly take the steps to achieve your desires and fulfill your purpose, blessings, and opportunities will start flooding in.

The purpose of this book is to help you destroy the mask you may be wearing and start to live a life of meaning and impact. In this book, I will help you break free from the things that cause you to live as someone you are not, empower you with the tools to start achieving the things you want to accomplish and tap into the power that lies within you.

I have taken strategies that were successful for me and am sharing them with you. The only way you can destroy your mask is if you go within. Take this journey seriously and take actionable steps to be who you were created to be. It is easy to live behind the mask and do what we think we are "supposed to do." But then we get to the end of our lives and reflect on missed opportunities, what we should have done, or who we should have been, and realize we didn't live up to our potential or lived a life that didn't serve us.

Everyone's journey is different, and each person will have different obstacles and opportunities along the way. I hope this book encourages and empowers you to take the next step in your journey. It is time to stop dreaming and start doing. It is time to stop playing it small and push through the fear so you can live in liberation. Destroying the mask is a form of rebirth. The journey is scary, but it is worth it.

You've got this, Queen!
With Love, Erin

Chapter 1:

TAKE INVENTORY*

In this book, Allah, the Creator, the Divine, and Source, are all names I use to describe God.

"We can't become what we need to be by remaining what we are."

— Oprah Winfrey

Everyone is born into a system. It could be a religious system, a belief system, a society heavily colonized or ruled by patriarchy, or some other structure. We were brought up with certain beliefs, and over time developed ways of thinking and being that were molded by the environment in which we were raised. As women, we are expected to grow up, meet the man, have kids, and care for the family. We are often taught to live life not as our own, but according to a standard and a mold of what a woman "should" be. In some environments, we were allowed to thrive and become who we were naturally supposed to be; other environments did not give us that opportunity due to conditioning and other factors. The core of who we are is often altered and shaped by societal and cultural expectations, and anything that varies from this "blueprint" is deemed unacceptable or rebellious.

WHAT BLUEPRINT WERE YOU TAUGHT TO FOLLOW?

Conditioning comes in various forms. In addition to gender roles, some of the conditioning includes the beauty standards our society dictates as desirable. So many women and young girls spend an enormous amount of money on beauty products and cosmetic surgeries, altering themselves and risking their lives because they are conditioned to think that a BBL or bigger breasts will make them beautiful. Another form of conditioning lies in the realm of career expectations, where we are frequently ingrained with the belief that certain educational and professional trajectories hold greater prestige while others are stigmatized or undervalued. This can influence an individual's career choices, pushing them towards certain paths and discouraging them from pursuing their true passions and living out their true purpose. Occasionally, conditioning molds us into individuals we were not inherently meant to be, diluting our true potential, and diverting us from our genuine selves. No matter the environment, we were all conditioned to some degree and developed patterns and attributes that formed our identity.

Acts 2:38 was the Scripture that molded my identity. *"Then Peter said unto them, Repent, and be baptized every one of you in the name of Jesus Christ for the remission of sins, and ye shall receive the gift of the Holy Ghost." (KJV)*

This was the cornerstone of my existence. This was my system, my lifeline, or so I thought. Believing anything outside of this scripture or the book of Acts was wrong. I believed that if this scripture was the center of my being, I would be okay. I would be saved. We would all be saved.

Let me back up and go to the beginning. I was born a Pentecostal Apostolic baby. From the time I was born, I was raised in church. The church was the major focus and priority of my life. I was part of a predominantly white Pentecostal organization that was founded in 1945. Growing up, there was a lack of spiritual leaders who shared my racial or ethnic background. However, within the organization, there existed an African American community that closely followed and admired the leaders, eagerly absorbing their teachings, despite occasionally encountering teachings that carried racist undertones. I will come back to this later.

In this organization, the book of Acts drives the core beliefs. Pentecostal Apostolics believe that to attain salvation, you must repent, be baptized in Jesus' name, and be filled with the Holy Ghost with the evidence of speaking in tongues. Believe in all of that, and you will be spared from eternal damnation. If only it were that easy. It is all simple until you read the fine print. The fine print is what gets you every time. You see, growing up in this denomination, there were a lot of things that you had to abide by so you wouldn't go to hell, even after you did everything according to Acts 2:38. The women could not wear pants, put on makeup, or cut their hair. The men had to be clean-shaven and had a lesser set of rules, but a set of guidelines either way. We were all carbon copies of one another. The church and its doctrine were our identity.

Even after being "saved," there were a lot of things that could send you to hell. According to this religion some of those things were not paying your tithes, violating any of The Ten Commandments, listening to secular music, going to the movies, dating someone outside of your race, religion, or denomination, disrespecting your parents, the list goes on. At times, it felt like there was no hope of getting to heaven because every Sunday, Wednesday, and Friday, the preacher's message would highlight all the things that were against God's will and plan. Even if you did all the things in Acts 2:38, your salvation was never guaranteed because if you went against anything in the fine print and did not repent of any sin before you died or before the rapture took place, you would still go to hell.

Exhausting right?

I was in constant paranoia trying to live perfectly and according to extremely specific rules just so I wouldn't spend my life in eternal damnation. Like other Christian denominations, we were subjected to teachings that implied certain consequences, such as illnesses or misfortune, if we didn't do things like, give a certain amount of money to the building fund, not take communion properly, or didn't comply with the rules that were established by the leadership.

Growing up in this denomination was a cult-like experience. We were told that no one outside of the Pentecostal Apostolic faith would see heaven. Even if they believed in God, went to church faithfully, and were good people, they would still go to hell because they did not follow the specific steps of salvation and did not follow the standards set by the denomination. We were taught that even though there were 40,000+ denominations of Christianity, our specific denomination was the only way.

This was all I knew. This was my foundation. This is what formed my identity. I lived in a fishbowl, a bubble. The only people I interacted with outside of the fishbowl were my family members who didn't go to this particular church. All I knew was this church. From kindergarten to 12th grade, I attended the church's school and never went to public school. I was educated with material that had a distorted view of reality and history. Just like many evangelical Christian denominations, it was dripped with white supremacy and patriarchy. It wasn't until I attended college that I learned about the real version of historical events. In college, my eyes slowly began to open to the real world and the possibilities around me.

There were great times living in "the fishbowl." I had friends, sang in the choir, and really had a passion for spreading God's message to the world. I believed in everything that I was taught. I believed that God was great and merciful, that he was the God of miracles, but also a God of wrath and punishment. When I think back on the way that I was taught to view God, at face value, God had a lot of narcissistic tendencies. He was a God that gave us free will, but if we didn't choose him we would suffer horrible consequences. While He was described as a God of love, grace, and mercy, any deviation from the prescribed path of the denomination was met with the expectation of fearing His wrath. I always felt anxious and unworthy. I did all the things I was supposed to do. Partly because I wanted to, but mostly because I didn't want to go to hell. I didn't wear pants, tried to keep my mind pure, and tried hard to be separate from the world because that was what we were supposed to do. I wanted to make God happy. I wanted to follow the blueprint.

When I started college, things began to change. The blueprint became blurry. At my church, what was once forbidden and not of God was suddenly allowed and "not a heaven or hell issue." The specific church I attended started moving away from the larger organization and out on its own. The Pentecostal doctrine did not change, but we could now wear pants, go to the movies, have TV, etc. Dating outside of your race or cutting your hair would no longer send you to hell. Things that we were told would have grave consequences, no longer had consequences. This entire time I was told I couldn't do it and now I can. What changed? For the first 20 years of my life, I was conditioned to believe these were some of the worst things you could do, but now they were deemed acceptable. This was where my foundation started to crack.

Buying my first pair of pants was a scary experience for me. Even though it was somewhat acceptable in my church, I still had people around me who believed pants and other things were wrong. I refused to wear them around church people and certain family members out of fear of being shunned or judged. I knew I was alright with God, but I didn't want to lose everyone else. I experienced this type of fear in many areas of my life. I was scared to do the wrong thing and fail God, scared to follow my passions because they didn't align with the church, and scared to attend another church of a different denomination because I was always taught that the Pentecostal Apostolic way was the only way. So, I just went through life doing what I thought I was supposed to do.

For years, I attended church because I thought I had to. I loved God, I loved "feeling the Spirit," I loved the music, and I enjoyed being encouraged by a positive sermon. If you asked me what I believed, I still quoted Acts 2:38, and in conversations about God, I blurted out scripture like a parrot; but when challenged, I couldn't give a rebuttal. I was a Christian, a Pentecostal. *How dare you question what I say?! I am of the chosen faith!*

That was the problem. I never questioned or truly examined any of it. Even when I had questions or doubts, I hurried those thoughts away because I was taught not to question God. Questioning God was yet another thing that would send you to hell. For years, I lived according to a blueprint I did not fully resonate with or embody. However, that all changed because of one name: George Floyd.

Fast forward to 2020. The COVID-19 pandemic quickly changed how we lived and went about life. We were faced with our mortality and were forced to live life a different way. Schools were closed, churches were closed, and we were confined to our homes whether we liked it or not. At the time, it was just my daughter and me. At first, I enjoyed the time I spent with her, the time I had to catch up on Netflix and finally do things around the house that I had been putting off. I was happy that I could work from home and did not have to worry about showing my face at church. By this point, I only attended so I could take my daughter to Sunday School and get some inspiration for the week. I was going through the motions. Just going to church on Sunday made me feel like I was still a "good Christian."

Everything was alright until the week George Floyd was killed. The country was divided and in turmoil, and emotions were high. That week, I needed some inspiration, so I tuned into an online church service. As I was listening to the message, the preacher, a White evangelical pastor of a church I frequented, totally missed the mark. Instead of comforting and encouraging the congregation, he added fuel to the fire. This "messenger of God" created even more division, resorted to spiritual bypassing, and even inserted politics in the message. I wasn't comforted or encouraged. I was outraged. I was sad and felt extremely hopeless. The foundation continued to crack. How could I continue blindly following these "people of faith?" How could I sit here under someone and an organization that lacks cultural sensitivity and compassion? How could I be spiritually led by people who can't even read the room? My entire life, I did what they said I should do. I believed in their "revelations from God." I held them high on a pedestal and allowed them to guide me. On this day, I began to allow myself to question everything I was taught to believe. I questioned everyone whom I was told to follow, and I vowed to figure out what was real, what I truly believed, and who God really was for me.

HAS SOMETHING EVER PROMPTED YOU TO TAKE INVENTORY OF YOUR BELIEFS?

Honestly, I didn't know where to start. At first, I felt like I had to find a new set of rules to follow or another system to tell me what I believed. I looked at other religions and Christian denominations, but I quickly became overwhelmed. They all started to run together. I then started writing down everything I was taught about God, things necessary for "salvation," and other items in the Pentecostal/evangelical blueprint; I took inventory of what I genuinely believed, and didn't believe, and made note of the areas where I was unsure.

I allowed myself to research the things I questioned instead of just believing what I was told. At times it was scary because I felt like I was "sinning," but I pushed through the fear and told myself that even if I came back to the blueprint I was given, I would not regret the journey of discovery. I knew God was real. I knew God was powerful. I wanted to experience God without the shackles of religion. My beginnings in the church introduced me to God and the power of God. While I hold immense gratitude for this, I quickly realized that I also had an extremely distorted view of God. I realized that I did not fully align with the version of Christianity that was presented to me, nor did I believe in everything that I was taught.

I wanted to get to know who God really was. I wanted to know who I really was. For years, my true essence poked through, but if anything did not align with the blueprint, I ignored it or pushed it away. This began my journey of transformation. The journey of removing the mask I was conditioned to wear. In this journey, I found that not only did I need to address the indoctrination of certain religious beliefs, but I also had to go through a bit of decolonization and examine and change the way I looked at myself as a Black woman. I needed to examine my foundation, figure out what I truly believed, and identify my core values.

We all have a foundation. My foundation was based on religion. Yours may be something different. To begin examining your foundation, it is crucial to achieve clarity by identifying your beliefs and non-beliefs, recognizing what resonates with you and what does not, and acknowledging areas where confusion exists. The way to do this is by going through the Inventory Process.

INVENTORY PROCESS

You can find the Inventory Process worksheet in your resource kit at the end of the book or by downloading the digital resource kit.

Take a sheet of paper and make three categories:
- Believe or Resonates
- Do Not Believe or Does not Resonate
- Unsure

Take time and allow yourself to take inventory of the things that make up your foundation. For example, you may believe that God exists, but are unsure whether your denomination or even Christianity is the only way to be "saved". Your culture and familial environment may have influenced your perspectives and instilled values or beliefs that do not currently align with you today. Whatever area, whatever item, big or small, identify them by placing them in their correct category. This process may take you an hour, a few days, or it may be an ongoing list that you add to and visit over time.

Once you've identified everything, begin researching the aspects you're unsure about. Take your time, as this does not have to be done all at once. Stay curious, and don't hesitate to ask questions of those you trust. If you feel overwhelmed, take a break and come back to it later. Researching for yourself helps you learn and make informed decisions.

Conditioning and indoctrination of any kind can have a ripple effect on our minds, the decisions we make for our lives, and the way we view the world around us. We all have our own story and unique journey, but many of us have the same outcomes. We end up living according to standards set by other people. We limit ourselves by conforming to narrow expectations, believing that we must adhere to certain norms, and therefore fall short of realizing our true potential. Perhaps the beliefs and values that have formed your identity no longer resonate and now feel forced. Perhaps you have gotten stuck living according to someone else's design and want to discover who you are at the core. Perhaps instead of doing what is expected of you, you have desires and feel called to do something totally different. Whatever the case, it is time to examine the foundation and identify the areas in your life that are misaligned.

Chapter 2:

ADDRESSING THE BAGGAGE

"Wanna fly, gotta give up the sh*t that weighs you down."

— *Toni Morrison*

Once you begin to examine your foundation and identify the things that serve and do not serve you, you may start to see the areas where you have developed viewpoints and ways of thinking that are not in your best interest and not in alignment with who you want to be. This may come up during times of meditation, times when you are triggered or challenged, or when you start to step out and accomplish your goals. Whether you are deconstructing from a religion or a certain way of being, you will have to let go of the baggage you accumulated during your life's journey. That baggage could be in the form of a set of beliefs or rules, limiting beliefs about yourself and others, specific viewpoints, habits, and the like. It is extremely difficult to let certain things go because they are entwined in your makeup and have defined who you are for some time. Letting things go is a continuous process.

Over time, you will evolve, and things that once served you will no longer be sufficient. The things you need to release will come up at different times throughout your life's journey. When they do, to remove the mask, you need to be equipped to release them.

Some of the things I needed to release came up when I started to visualize myself doing what I dreamed of or things I felt called to do. Every time I saw myself doing something positive, a negative thought would come up about how I'd never be able to do it or how I wasn't worthy. I felt like I was either too big, too black, too dumb, or too ugly to receive or do what I wanted to do. Low self-esteem and depression were baggage that I needed to deal with. I needed to decolonize my mind and unpack the way I was taught to view my blackness and my beauty.

I grew up a thick black girl in a predominately white space and never thought that my blackness was good enough. To me, being black was viewed as less than. If I acted a certain way, I would be accepted. But if I spoke too loudly or acted "too ghetto," there would be problems. Deep down, I loved being black and loved my culture. However, whenever I expressed my love for my culture and people, I would be laughed at or made to feel like I was weird. So, I just tried to conform and be a "good black," a black that wasn't problematic or too outspoken.

As a teenager, I often tried to conform to the white beauty standards within my church organization, and society. My natural hair was not seen as beautiful, so I kept it straightened and relaxed. I heavily edited myself, how I spoke, and how I acted to better align with the people around me. Many of the girls I grew up with were skinny and white, so I developed a bit of self-hatred because I didn't fit the mold. To me, they were the standard.

I also dealt with low self-esteem. Due to some complications at birth, I was left with hands and feet that were cosmetically different from everyone else. Growing up, I felt like God made a mistake or that because He didn't love me, He made me less than – a cheap counterfeit of a real human. I carried these feelings into my adult- . hood, and it affected the way I viewed myself, how I allowed people to treat me, and what I felt like I could or couldn't accomplish. Negative and limiting beliefs have a bigger impact on our lives than we think or care to admit. They can set the trajectory for our success or failure. I realized this right after I contemplated suicide.

The first time I thought about suicide, I was about 13 years old. It actually became a habit. Whenever my depression got really bad or something major happened, the thought of suicide would comfort me. The thought of ending it all would make me feel so much better. I took this habit into adulthood. I had relationships that were toxic and I accepted treatment that I shouldn't have because of the way I viewed myself. Several years after I had my daughter, I let someone into my life that did not value me and took advantage of me. Having dealt with loneliness and not wanting to go through it again, I held on to the man and I told myself I was going to make it work regardless of how he treated me. I felt like I deserved the poor treatment because of who I was. I truly believed that I was not enough and that I needed to take what I could get. This way of thinking almost killed me.

One day, after being made aware of his deceptive actions, I had enough and ended things. I started blaming myself for letting him make a fool of me, I was angry because I was alone again, and I felt disgusting. I felt unworthy of the type of love I desired. The negative talk continued and in my foggy haze of sadness and despair, my old habit kicked in – I wanted to end it. I wanted to end it many times before in the past, but this time, I had a plan. I was scared. I felt myself spiraling out of control and the only thing that anchored me was my daughter. I thought about her as she slept in the next room. I never wanted her to be here without me and I realized that if I did not get the help I needed, she would not have a mother.

Thankfully, I had enough sense to call to the suicide hotline and the person on the other side of the call talked me down just enough to get out of the haze I was in and encouraged me to immediately call my therapist who I trusted at the time. That night she answered my call and after talking to her, I was able to get out of the danger zone and begin the journey of doing the work to tackle the negative and limiting beliefs I had about myself. For a long time, I allowed my limiting beliefs to run my life. Those beliefs affected the way I presented myself, the jobs I took, the experiences I denied myself, and the people I allowed into my life.

HOW DO LIMITING BELIEFS SHOW UP IN YOUR LIFE?

Limiting beliefs manifest in different ways; they can take the form of an inner voice that discourages you or your abilities, or they can be beliefs you have gradually internalized over time. These beliefs will contribute to us wearing a mask and showing up as a watered-down and stifled version of ourselves. Some examples of limiting beliefs are:

- "I am not good enough to do that."
- "I could never make that much money."
- "I don't deserve success or happiness."
- "That type of love only exists for other people."

- "Why should I even try? I'm going to fail anyway."
- "She is prettier and skinnier. Why would he ever be interested in me?"

You are what you believe you are. If you believe you aren't worthy of love, you will most likely attract people who won't love you fully and completely. If you believe you can't, you most likely won't. I had TONS of limiting beliefs. My head used to be filled with negative thoughts about myself. I constantly told myself I was less than and accepted less because that was what I thought I deserved. In addition to dating men who were extremely disrespectful, I never spoke up for myself at work; I didn't even buy things that I wanted because I felt like I wasn't good enough to have them. My limiting beliefs ran my life until I made the conscious effort to combat them and reprogram the way I thought. When you tell yourself something, whether it is true or not, your brain will accept it as truth. What limiting beliefs are holding you back from living the life you desire?

Here are 5 ways to tackle limiting beliefs:

1. Identify the belief: Become aware of the specific belief that is holding you back. Acknowledge its presence and the impact it has on your life.

2. Challenge the belief: Question the validity of the belief. We often tell ourselves a story in our head and believe it to be true. Ask yourself if this belief is based on facts or if it's simply your perception.

3. Replace your limiting beliefs with empowering beliefs: Replace the limiting belief with a positive and empowering belief that counteracts it. Choose beliefs that align with your goals, values, and who you are. As soon as you have the thought, "I can't," combat that thought by saying things like, "I can," "I can do hard things," and "I am fully supported."

4. Practice positive affirmations: Use positive affirmations to reinforce the new empowering beliefs. Repeat affirmations daily that counteract the limiting belief regularly and rewire the negative thinking patterns you have developed over time.

5: Journaling and self-reflection: Engage in journaling or self-reflection exercises to explore the origins of your limiting beliefs. Make the conscious choice to unlearn and let go of beliefs that no longer serve you. You can find Journal Prompts and Self-Reflection Questions in your resource kit at the end of the book or by downloading the digital resource kit.

Limiting beliefs are only one form of baggage, and baggage can manifest in different ways. When you realize that it is time to let things go, the following additional steps can help you release the baggage so your rebirth can begin, and the mask can be destroyed.

#1 Forgiveness

Forgiveness is extremely important in this process because as you begin to dig deep, you may find areas where you need to forgive yourself and others. Once I deconstructed and during my times of shadow work, I was able to see the areas in which I was not a good human being. Growing up, I was extremely hard-core for Christ and shunned and looked down on people who didn't have the same beliefs as I did. What is the saying? There is no hate like Christian love. Yeah, that is a true statement. In other areas, I noticed that I wasn't the best at controlling my anger and frustration (still a struggle) and would say or do things that hurt other people. Upon these realizations, I felt disgusted with who I was. I still cringe at the things I did as a teenager and young adult in the name of God and my religion. If you knew me back then, please accept my apology. I was a mess. Many of us are a product of our environment, and we will never see the true picture unless we make a conscious effort to see through a clear lens. Once I saw the true picture, I had to forgive myself.

Forgiving yourself feels so much harder than forgiving others. You feel sorrow deep down in your soul, and you constantly think about what you should have done. Shame and guilt can eat away at you and put you in a self-loathing prison. You cannot experience true rebirth and peace if you do not forgive yourself. No one is perfect. Acknowledge the mistakes, take ownership, give yourself grace, and release yourself of guilt and shame.

As I was beginning this process, I realized that I held on to resentment from not forgiving various people in my life. Wounds that occurred as a child and teenager were still fresh, as well as things that were done to me as an adult. I carried the trauma around like it was armor. I realized that by not forgiving, I was hurting myself more than others. I was the one walking around suffering, and the people that hurt me were living their lives like nothing happened. The term "forgive and forget" never sat right with me because one thing I'll NEVER do is forget. You can remember what people did; in fact, I wholeheartedly believe when you remember, it helps you to maneuver situations in the future. However, you do not have to be a slave to what someone did to you. If you are hurt, broken or shattered, do what you must to find peace despite what others have done. Whether you are forgiving yourself or someone else, forgiveness is a choice. A choice that is necessary if rebirth is what you desire.

#2 Address Fear

Fear can stem from limiting beliefs or from other people. When you encounter fear, ask yourself this question, "Is this my fear, or was this fear given to me?" A lot of the fear that I had was given to me. I was taught to fear things because of the threat of hell or other reasons that originated in someone else. Other fears that I had stemmed from not knowing the outcome of a situation. I found that I said no to a lot of things because of this. Fear can be so crippling. It is natural to be scared and worried about the journey, but once you learn to do it scared and walk through the fear, there is no looking back.

#3 Embrace New

As you are forgiving, tackling limiting beliefs, and addressing your fears, start embracing the new. Embrace your goals, the blessings that life brings, and the divine messages given to you by the Creator. Open your heart to what is for you and live according to your authentic self. If something lights you up, go deeper. If you are drawn to something, follow its path. Follow the nudges and the calling of your purpose. Destroying the mask is allowing yourself to let go of the old and live a life that honors who you truly are and what you are called to do.

Chapter 3:

THE TIGHTROPE EXPERIENCE

"It always seems impossible until it is done."

— *Nelson Mandela*

During the beginning of my deconstruction experience, I started to make it a habit to meditate. I had always been interested in meditation, but never took it seriously because when I tried, my thoughts were everywhere, and I felt like I'd never "get it." However, after being consistent and researching several types of meditation practices and methods, I was able to find my flow. I made it a point to meditate for at least 20 minutes a day; some days, I would meditate for an hour. It was during this time that I realized that growing up Christian we were taught to pray and ask God for things, but we were never really taught to listen. Through intentional meditation, I learned how to listen for the answers I sought, listen to warnings, and listen for the direction I needed to take.

I was a few months into my journey, and I had already established that I wanted to live by who I felt I was and that I would do the things I'd either been wanting to do or be open to the things that God had for me. I had written about ten things on my vision board that I wanted to achieve. Many of these items had been on my board for years, but I had never gotten close to achieving them. There were things on there that I had always dreamed of having and/or doing but felt like I would never receive due to limiting beliefs, inherited fear, or the size of the goal. I was at the point where I was willing to put it all out there and actively work so I could achieve at least one or two of my goals.

There were also things not included on the vision board that I felt compelled to pursue, like starting a business, interests that weren't considered normal, etc. However, I refrained from adding them due to my Type A personality, which needed to know the why, the how, and the what at all times. I've always been the type of person who needs to know every single step of the process before I make any decision. I need to weigh the pros and cons. I need to know what it will be like before I do it, and I need a detailed account of the proposed outcome. So, while certain things were heavy on my heart, I wouldn't let my mind completely entertain them because I couldn't see the process or the outcome. This all changed once I had my tightrope experience.

There were a few things that were in my heart to explore, and I kept brushing them off. During this particular week, I was thinking about them heavily and decided to write about them in my journal to just get them out of my system so I could focus on my day. Later that day, I was confronted with the feelings again when I heard someone talking on a podcast about one of the items I wrote in my journal. I cried and cried because it was something that I wanted to do deep down, but it came with a lot of fear and uncertainty. I didn't know how it was going to happen, or what it was going to look like, but I just knew deep in my soul that it was for me. Once I put my daughter to bed, I decided to meditate. I'd been avoiding talking about it or praying about it, but on this night, I decided to stop running.

I lit some incense and candles, turned on some music, and started to meditate. At the beginning of the meditation, I set the intention to be open to whatever messages I received and to try to have some sort of peace about the decisions I would make. I had been meditating for about 15-20 minutes and suddenly in my mind, I saw myself on a cliff. A wall was behind me, and I was on the ledge. When I looked down, it looked like I was over the Grand Canyon. The rocks had beautiful shades of orange and brown. I was surrounded by beauty, and I was up extremely high in the air. As I was looking around, I was holding on to the wall and saw a tightrope in front of me when I looked down again. The tightrope was long and crossed over a huge area of rocks below. It was so long I couldn't even see the other side. I then heard a voice telling me to cross. I immediately knew it was God. The voice was coming from the other side, and it kept telling me to cross. As I looked down, I became scared and nervous because it was too high. I pressed harder into the wall behind me and told God that I was scared, and I wouldn't be able to do it. The voice was insistent and kept telling me to cross. At this point, I put my foot on the tightrope but still held on to the wall. Shaking and scared, I told God that I could not go any further because I would have to let go of the wall and would have nothing to hold on to. Then the voice said, "That's the point. You must let go of the wall and trust that you are supported to make it to the other side." I immediately snapped out of that experience and cried like a baby for the rest of the meditation.

That night, I received the full realization that whatever I am being called to do, I am supported the entire way and loved in the process. All the times I wanted to take a chance but played it small, I would have been supported. All the times that I had an idea or a dream but succumbed to the fear of others, I would have been supported. The time I wasted. The opportunities I missed. The paths that I avoided. I would have been supported.

Never will I play it small again. Never will I allow fear to stop me from doing what I am purposed to do. I will do it scared before I choose not to do it at all. It was that night that I decided to go all in on my dreams. I decided that I would live unapologetically and authentically in alignment with what I felt like I was supposed to do and who I was supposed to be.

Most of the time, we will not see the entire journey. We will only see just enough to take the next step. The tightrope may be shaky and scary, but you are supported the entire way.

Where are you on your tightrope? Are you still holding on to the wall, or are you making your way across, knowing that you will be supported the entire way? Living a divinely inspired life is like walking on a tightrope. We are challenged to cross with full reliance on the wisdom and direction of God.

At the beginning of my deconstruction journey, I felt like a piece of paper that was blowing in the wind. Deconstructing your beliefs is not for the weak. During the process, there will be times when you feel lost, like a ship drifting on the sea in a storm. All your life, you have been given a set of rules, adopted various beliefs and mentalities, and have lived according to the precepts of others. You may have viewed the world through a distorted lens. At least, I did. The way I viewed myself, the world, and God was from inside of a rose-colored box. A box where everything I saw was the same shade and had the same biased view. Deconstruction took me out of that box, and I finally saw the true colors of life. I finally saw other things that were available to me: different beliefs, different viewpoints, different ways of being. I was no longer a prisoner of religion and unnatural ways of thinking. Even though I was out of the box, I felt overwhelmed and lacked direction. All the core values and things I lived my life by no longer applied. I was the driver of my ship, and now I didn't know where to go. I felt like a ship without a sail. A ship without an anchor.

During the deconstruction process, it is easy to fall into another set of beliefs or organized ways of thinking because you are used to being told what to do and what to think. After you take inventory of what you believe and do not believe, what serves you versus what does not, you will need something to ground you when the water gets rough. This is where your anchor comes in. During this journey, you may find that you better align with the principles and teachings of another group, and that is beautiful. You may also find that the principles resonating with you do not fully align with one group or organization, and that is fine too. As you explore and learn, there is a process that I would like to walk you through to come up with your core values. Core values are the deeply held principles that guide your choices, shape your relationships, and guide your approach to problem-solving$_1$. These core values will serve as your anchor as you navigate the journey on your tightrope.

Step 1: Answer the following questions:

1. Based on what you have learned about yourself and what resonates with you, how do you want to show up in the world?

2. What values or virtues do you now prioritize or want to prioritize in your relationships, work, and personal life?
3. What values would best support your well-being, self-care, and overall mental, emotional, and physical health?
4. What are some signs or feelings that something is in alignment with your true self?
5. Which fundamental principles and values from your upbringing would you like to preserve and carry forward in your journey?

If you find it helpful, feel free to refer to a list of values in your resource kit at the end of the book while exploring and identifying your core values.

Step #2 -Identify your top 3 values

These values will be your anchor and the blueprint you live your life by. These values may change over time but will serve as a compass for living a more authentic and purposeful life. When selecting my core values, I intentionally chose peace, success, and liberation. These values serve as compass points for me, guiding my choices and actions. If a relationship, opportunity, or endeavor lacks a sense of peace, I recognize that it may not align with my path. Similarly, if it does not contribute to my personal growth and success, I understand that it may not be the right fit. Lastly, I prioritize my authenticity and refuse to subject myself to situations where I feel restricted or unable to be my true self.

Whatever your core values are, be sure that they truly align with who you are and not who you are told to be. Ensure that they can be your guiding force as you navigate your way through the journey of the unknown. If something comes up and does not align with your values, then it is not for you. Trust the process and know that you are supported every step of the way.

Chapter 4:

LISTEN TO YOUR INTUITION

"If your soul is on fire to serve in a way that scares you to death. And you don't feel worthy, ready, able. And the burning will not leave you alone. Congratulations. You have your calling."

– Jaiya John

ntuition is defined as *"an ability to understand or know something immediately based on your feelings rather than facts.*$_2$*"* They always say a woman's intuition is always right and that we need to trust it if we feel something is off. This saying is mostly used when trying to figure out if our man or someone in our circle is being truthful or not. Many times, we can use our intuition as an investigative compass about others but fail to know how to use it when it comes to ourselves. Our intuition is a valuable tool on this journey of discovery. In your own 'tightrope experience' and journey, following your intuition is one of the most important components in the process. It will keep you from falling off the rope, it will protect you from harmful paths or people that are not for you, and it will help you avoid making the wrong decisions.

We all have intuition – choosing to listen is the key. I feel like our intuition can be used as a compass in our journey of life. I feel our intuition is a version of God's voice. It is the most important voice, but also the quietest. How many times have you listened to your intuition and been correct? How many times has your intuition told you to go left, but everyone is going right? How many times have you said, "I should have listened to my intuition?" We all have it, but oftentimes, our intuition is obstructed by the influence of our ego or the ingrained programming and conditioning we have absorbed from different systems and sources throughout our lives. For most of my adult life, I listened to the voice of my anxiety and my ego. The voice of my anxiety was driven by fear. I grew up in fear. Fear that if I made one wrong move, I would go to hell, invoke God's wrath, or receive unbearable consequences because of my choice. This stuck with me for a long time. Every time I wanted to try something new, have a new experience or do something a different way, a voice would intervene and give me all the reasons I shouldn't or couldn't do it. This voice was loud and kept me paralyzed. My ego often interfered as well. I often compared myself to others and then told myself that I wasn't the type of person who could achieve or have certain things. Does this sound familiar?

When people talk about ego, they usually say that someone is full of themselves or thinks more highly of themselves. However, the ego is how we identify ourselves and who we believe we are at our core. Our ego also has positive attributes and can help keep us safe. However, there are also negative sides to our ego. According to Owen Lloyd, the ego holds all our fears, doubts, and insecurities, and it's what causes us to believe we are better or less than other human beings$_3$. How has your ego shown up in your life? In what ways does your ego control or overshadow your intuition?

To cancel out or minimize negative and inhibiting voices, we must first be able to identify what voices we are listening to and strengthen our intuition to be able to hear that small, still voice telling us what to do and where to go. Here are some signs that indicate when our ego, fear, or other unnecessary voices are speaking instead of our intuition:

1. Fear-based thoughts: These thoughts often come as worst-case scenarios and fabricated stories we tell ourselves with extremely negative outcomes.

2. Overthinking: The mind becomes overwhelmed with thoughts and excessive analysis. These thoughts usually keep us paralyzed.

3. Need for external validation: We don't usually trust ourselves or our intuition, so we run to others to confirm or deny our thoughts. While seeking wise counsel is beneficial in many situations, others still may not have the same insight or message we have received from Source. Be careful about seeking validation from someone who has no business having access to your journey and the instructions you have been given.

4. Judgment and comparison: We find ourselves comparing ourselves to other people, believing that we must possess the same attributes as them, and then judging ourselves for falling short.

5. Impatience: Our anxiety and fear sometimes make us feel like we aren't doing things fast enough or that we need to

make hasty decisions instead of taking our time to process and gain a deeper understanding of what we are supposed to do. The fear of missing out often drives us to make quick and ill-informed decisions.

Have you experienced any of these? Have these thoughts interrupted your intuition? Our intuition should bring us peace. Here are some signs that your intuition is speaking to you:

1. Deep inner peace and resonance: When you consider a certain path or decision, you feel a profound sense of inner peace, alignment, or resonance. It feels right at a deeper level, even if it may not make immediate sense to the rational mind.

2. Clarity and simplicity: The messages or nudges we receive are usually direct, simple, and clear. Intuition is devoid of mental clutter and overwhelm.

3. Gut instinct: Often, our intuition comes as a deep sense of knowing or "gut feeling" about a situation or decision, sometimes without being able to provide a logical explanation.

4. Increased flow: When you follow your intuition, you may notice that events and opportunities seem to align effortlessly, and things flow more smoothly. It feels as if you are supported in your journey.

How does your intuition show up for you?

To begin destroying the mask, you must be divinely led and have the ability to cancel out voices that do not serve you. Take time to get better connected to the Source and take intentional steps to strengthen your intuition. The following activities can be done to strengthen your intuition[4]:

1. Meditation: Meditation is the most critical component to strengthen your intuition. It provides you with time to self-reflect, be still, and be able to process thoughts or better interpret the messages you may be receiving.

2. Do a body scan: Your intuition can speak to you through your body. At times, it may feel like a tugging at your heart or in your belly. The more you become in tune with your body, the more sensitive you become to your intuition. Try to identify what confirmation feels like. Pay attention if you get uncomfortable or have a negative sensation in your body when trying to make a decision. Try to figure out if this feeling is fear, limiting beliefs, or your intuition telling you not to proceed.

3. Rest and disconnect: We all become busy and have lives that keep us on the go. Our responsibilities can often keep us from paying attention to our intuition and hinder our progress because we do not take the time to focus on things we need to focus on. Take intentional time to slow down, rest your mind, and disconnect from technology and people who may be distracting you.

4. Lean in: Allow yourself to feel and listen to what is coming through. We often try to ignore, resist, and push past what we are feeling instead of allowing ourselves to lean into what we feel or know. Commit to being present and intentionally listen to what your intuition is telling you.

Chapter 5:

TURNING DREAMS INTO REALITY

"Be careful what you set your heart upon for it will surely be yours."

— James Baldwin

A s a child, to escape my reality, I created extremely detailed alternate realities in my head and often envisioned myself in a different life doing things that I thought would bring me joy. Whenever I became sad, upset, or bored, I would turn to my alternate world, and it would bring me comfort. I would escape who I was forced to be and envision living a life having experiences that were forbidden in my community and doing things I was naturally drawn to. First, it started as me imagining myself grown and going to work in a pantsuit with red lipstick on and a cute haircut. This may seem basic, but I was told that all of that was wrong. This habit stuck with me into adulthood. Whenever times got tough, or I experienced struggle, I would imagine myself in the life I truly desired and as the person I wanted to be. When I was single and/or lonely, I would often imagine the type of man I desired and what types of things I'd want us to experience together. When I was dissatisfied with other things in my life, I envisioned myself living in a new place, working a job I loved, and living a life where I could be myself and do the things I always wanted to do. At some point, I realized these alternate realities I imagined myself in were not just figments of my imagination; they were real desires and goals. I would dream of myself traveling the world, falling in love, having businesses, making an impact, and living as an unedited version of myself – but I didn't think that I could have access to that life.

When you have grown up in a repressive system, sometimes you become brainwashed or conditioned to think that you can't do certain things, or that you have to live a specific type of lifestyle to be deemed acceptable or worthy. You may have dreams and desires but are suppressing them out of the conditioning you have experienced. You may feel called to do something, but because it goes against the rules or guidelines of your system, you ignore the pull. Is there a dream or desire that is poking through that you just cannot get out of your head? Do you envision yourself living a different life or doing something totally new? I am here to tell you, do not ignore it. Lean into your dreams, for they may be connected to your purpose and the experiences you are supposed to have.

During the early phase of my journey, I asked myself, "What if? What if I could do the things I always wanted to do? What if I could have some of the experiences I've conjured up in my alternate realities?" After years of denying my desires and ignoring certain callings, I allowed myself to truly entertain what it would look and feel like to do the things I wanted to do. I no longer look at my dreams as just dreams. Once I allowed myself to clearly see the vision without my limiting beliefs, negative voices, or stories getting in the way, I began to craft the vision.

To actualize your dreams, you must see your dreams and visions as tangible goals. As soon as I realized this, I started to write down everything that I wanted to do, no matter how big or small, and what it would look like once I accomplished my goals. This is the first step in turning your visions into reality.

What do you want to do? What do you feel called to do?

Here is an activity that can get you started:

Set aside some time when you will be undisturbed. Give yourself at least 20 minutes to an hour for this activity. Take out a sheet of paper, turn on some music, make your space extremely comfortable, and just start dreaming. All the things that are in your head, all the things that you want to do, start writing them down. It doesn't have to be in any specific order; just start writing them down and put your vision on paper.

Let's say you don't have dreams per se, but you are experiencing a calling or feeling drawn to do something, write down exactly what it is you are being pulled to do or explore. You may not know why or understand it at the time, but that "thing" may be something you need to research and explore further. It may help point you in the direction you are supposed to go and can be used as a bridge or catalyst to connect the dots in your journey.

Once you are finished writing everything out, read what you wrote down and add more. Get out everything that you've been keeping in your head no matter how big or small. Once you are done, do not share this list with anyone else. This list will be your guide and your compass as to where you will put your energy and what you will focus on for the next three months to two years, or however long it takes for you to achieve them.

When doing this activity, it is extremely beneficial for you to be detailed. Outline exactly what you want. Don't just write down *a house*. Instead, write *a house with a backyard and pool, a deck, at least three bedrooms, and a big kitchen.* Get extremely specific and identify what you want. Your limiting beliefs will want you to play it small and will tell you that your dreams are too big. Do not allow your limiting beliefs to get in the way; push through them and identify exactly what you want. If you want to get your degree but don't know how that is going to happen, it doesn't matter. If you want to live abroad, have four kids, or take a trip but don't know how you would be able to do that, it does not matter. Write it down. You do not need to know 'the how' right now; just focus on 'the what'. Allow yourself to dream, allow yourself to get excited, and give yourself permission to make your dreams a reality.

You can find the Dreams to Reality worksheet in your resource kit. You can use this document to write down any dreams, goals, or callings you have.

Chapter 6:

THE TRUTH ABOUT MANIFESTATION

"Every great dream begins with a dreamer. Always remember you have within you the strength, the patience, and the passion to reach for the stars to change the world."

– Harriet Tubman

After identifying exactly what I wanted to do and writing down all the things that I wanted to accomplish, I started researching how to bring them to pass. My research led me to manifestation. This is a buzzword that has been floating around lately in different spiritual communities, and I've heard it used in the evangelical church as well. Gurus of today tell you that you can manifest anything you want in a quick amount of time. They make it seem that you can manifest that job, that man, that $1,500 purse in just a matter of weeks or days. While I do believe things can happen quickly, in my opinion manifestation does not work like that. At times, I feel that manifestation is used as an attempt to bypass the work that must be done. Just like we sometimes try to use prayer alone to avoid responsibility.

Growing up, we were taught to pray for miracles and things that we wanted, and God, like a magician, would grant us our wish without us having to do anything at all. We would quote, "*Faith without works is dead,*" but would miss the work part. This is how we treat manifestation. We treat it as some magical tool that will bring us all the riches and desires in the world without having to lift a finger.

At the beginning of my journey, I researched several ways to manifest. You had scripting, the 369 method, prayers, various moon rituals, sex, and the list goes on. I tried to figure out what was best for me, and which would bring me what I wanted in the quickest way. I was left disappointed many times because I didn't get the job that I was trying to manifest, or the relationship that I thought I manifested didn't turn out as planned. I solely relied on the tool to bring me what I wanted. Through the disappointment, I painfully realized that manifestation requires more than my desire and a ritual. Manifestation requires work. To truly manifest, there are certain things you must do outside of a ritual to make it happen.

The first step you must take is to be sure the thing you want is in alignment with what you truly desire or feel led to do. A new job was on my list of things I desired. However, I was applying for jobs that were not in alignment with what I really wanted to do. I was applying for school principal jobs because that was the next logical step for me in my career, but I truly did not want to be a principal. I was too scared to apply for jobs outside of the school district. I ignored the pings in my heart to look in other directions because I thought that being a principal would make sense. I'd do a manifestation ritual, apply for the job, get a call for an interview, and feel so accomplished because I just knew I had manifested this opportunity. I'd interview and would be devastated because I didn't get the job. I'd be so upset because I thought that I had done all the things to manifest this job and was left to look for something else.

I repeated this a few times and was left feeling confused and hurt. Finally, I turned inward and got in alignment with what I truly desired. I opened myself up to take a chance and apply for opportunities that were outside of my comfort zone. The doors of opportunity started to open.

Each one of us has a unique calling, and when we choose to align with our true selves, we can more effectively manifest our desires because they are meant for us, rather than pursuing things that ultimately won't serve us. God, Allah, the Creator knows what we need and what we truly desire.

The next step to manifestation is belief. This is probably the most crucial step. If you don't believe that you can have or do something, you most likely will not have it and will not do it! You can say all the things and write what you would like to manifest a hundred times on a piece of paper, but if you don't believe it, you have wasted your time and energy. Believing is seeing it and feeling it in your core. Speaking as if it were already done. This is where visualizations and affirmations come into the manifestation process.

If you want to be a boss, see yourself as a boss. What does it look like? What does it feel like? What does a boss do? Visualize it and get into the energy of a boss. Affirm that you are already a boss and that you have what it takes to do the job. When I wanted to move out of my hometown, I visualized myself thriving in another place, with different people and giving my daughter an atmosphere filled with distinct cultures and diverse backgrounds. So, I started doing things that embodied the move; I adopted the energy of moving and starting fresh. I did not have a job lined up. I was applying for jobs in numerous cities. I received rejections left and right, but I knew that I would be moving. I knew that I would have an opportunity.

Lastly, manifestation requires inspired action. While there are things that only God can provide, we have the responsibility to take the necessary steps to be prepared to do and receive the things we desire. Look at the dreams or goals you listed in the previous chapter. Identify what you would like to accomplish first. What steps would you have to take to have that thing you desire, or how can you prepare yourself to receive what you desire?

Use the following activity and create an action plan:

Choose three to five items on your list that you will focus on first. Now, choose one dream and make a list of everything you would need to do to prepare to receive it. Then work backwards.

Let's say you want a house. The house is the desired outcome. Start thinking about what you must do to buy the house. Do you need to repair your credit? Do you need to research first-time home buyer programs? Do you need to create a budget and start saving for a down payment?

Not only do we need to make physical preparations, but energetic ones as well. Do you want a relationship? Assess the things you would need to do to prepare to receive a person in your life. Do you need to go to therapy and work on trauma from the past?

Do you need to change habits and work on your mindset? Do you need to start putting yourself in situations where you can meet people and have new social experiences? If you don't have the energetic or emotional capacity to receive or give love, when a person comes along who would be a good fit, you will not be able to receive or keep them because you aren't in the place you need to be.

There are times when we pray for things but never receive them because we are not ready or equipped to have them. Manifestation is not a magic trick. It is truly believing that you can have what you desire and taking the necessary steps for it to come to pass.

When I listed out every dream and/or goal on my vision list, I had about fifteen items. I concentrated on 3-5 at a time. The major items were:

1. Get a new job out of the classroom or school that still aligns with education.

2. Move to a new state with a great arts scene and diverse population.

3. Be open to finding love.

4. Have a house with a nice deck and a backyard.

5. Visit Africa – any country, but preferably West Africa.

First, I focused on getting a new job and moving. I knew that moving was in alignment with my desire and purpose, so I started doing the things that were necessary for my desires to come to pass. While I didn't know where I was going or what job I would be taking, I believed and knew that I would be moving, so I began to prepare. I decluttered my house and got rid of everything I was not using. I cleaned my basement and prepared my house for sale or rental so when the time came for me to leave, I would be ready.

I even started putting things I was not using in boxes. About six months before this, I started improving my credit. I knew that eventually, I would want another house, even if it was in my hometown. I began to save money, do research, and act as if I was going to move even though I didn't know where I was going. I did the work. I truly believe that when you know what you are supposed to do and do the work, God will meet you where you are and make things happen.

Some months after I started getting my house in order, I found love, received a job offer in another state, and put my house up for sale. My house was on the market for only two weeks, and I was living in my new state a month later. Had I not prepared, I don't think I would have been able to move so quickly. I was able to manifest the job, the move, and a good school for my daughter. Five months after my move, I was able to purchase my home with my backyard and deck. It felt like a whirlwind! Within a year and a half, I not only visited West Africa, but I was also able to receive dual citizenship in Sierra Leone, the home of my maternal ancestors.

What is for you, is for you! There will be times when things will just happen without you having to do anything. But for other things, if you are in alignment with who you are, believe that you can, and take inspired actions, God will meet you where you are, and the doors of opportunities will be open for you. Not only can you receive exactly what you desire, but your desires can act as a catalyst to push you into accomplishing things you never imagined.

You can find the Prepare for the Manifestation worksheet in your resource kit.

Chapter 7:
_____

DETERMINE YOUR IMPACT

*"A life is not important except in the impact it
has on other lives."*

— *Jackie Robinson*

I wrote this book to help women understand that they can show up as their true selves, have the life they desire, and leave an impactful legacy. You may ask what legacy has to do with this. Legacy has EVERYTHING to do with it. Let me tell you how.

In my bio, you may have read that I am a Rebirth-to-Death Doula. In my work, I aim to help women have a transformative rebirth, help them live with audacity, and leave a legacy. There are different types of death doulas, and they work in different capacities. Some death doulas help people prepare for the inevitable end by helping them get their advanced directives together, helping them plan for funerals, writing wills, and doing legacy work. Other doulas will help you through the dying process. They may sit by your side as you die. They may support the family by helping them take care of you, your final moments, and the moments immediately after your passing. Other doulas may help wrap things up after a loved one passes away. They may help close out accounts, contact the proper people to tell them that you have passed away and they may help with grief services, etc.

I wanted to become a death doula after having an extreme interest in death and the afterlife. I never really shared this with anyone, but all my life, I was interested in all things related to death and knew that I wanted to work in this field in some way. I just never knew what it would look like.

Death is an interesting concept in Western society. As Americans, we are so obsessed with death. Crime shows are the most popular shows on TV. True crime podcasts are one of the highest-ranking genres in podcasts, and listeners consume death and murder for hours as a pastime activity. I am a true crime fan and have listened to countless hours of media dealing with murder and destruction. In my opinion, we have become so used to death, that now, we don't flinch or ask any questions when there is a mass shooting. It feels like we have accepted them as the norm and can easily listen to hours of news coverage describing deaths in detail as we eat our dinner and spend time with our families. However, when death comes to our doorstep, and we are personally greeted with it or even the possibility of it, that is when we don't want anything to do with it. Suddenly, a phobia arises, and we run away in fear.

If you are alive right now, there is a 100% chance that you will die. These statistics will never change. The minute we are born, death is the only thing that is guaranteed. We all know this but still live like we have all the time in the world and fail to live up to the potential we are born with. We waste our time doing other things instead of doing what we have been designed to do, or we waste time living as someone we are not.

Are you using this life to do what you are supposed to do?
Are you wasting time and showing up as someone else and not
truly enjoying it as your authentic self?

Often, we don't realize a person's impact until they are gone. When someone dies, we always hear about how special they were, learn about different things they did for others, and can truly see the effect they had on the people around them. Each of us was born to have an impact on others. Our life's mission is never for us; it is to impact those around us and those who come after us. I often think about the great leaders and changers of the past like Dr. Martin Luther King Jr., Harriet Tubman, Malcolm X, and Rosa Parks, whose impact is still felt after their ascension.

Dr. Rebecca Lee Crumpler was the first African American woman to earn an M.D. degree. She was born in 1835 and worked as a nurse before defying the odds and becoming a doctor, and the first African American to have a medical publication. Her journey started with a passion. She has been quoted saying, *"I early conceived a liking for, and sought every opportunity to relieve the sufferings of others*5*."* Dr. Crumpler was born into a system just like many of the greats I mentioned before. In this deeply entrenched system, African Americans were systematically devalued, denied their fundamental human rights, and deprived of access to education on equal terms with their white counterparts. We were subjected to a dehumanizing existence, conditioned to feel inferior and subservient, and subjected to the despicable treatment reminiscent of mere livestock in the fields. Dr. Crumpler could have been a product of her environment, but instead she followed the dreams and nudges that would catapult her to living in her purpose and making an impact on aspiring doctors who came after her.

I firmly believe that your dreams and who you are at your core are intricately woven into the fabric of your purpose and the unique experiences you are supposed to have during your journey in this lifetime. There is a reason you feel called to do "that thing." Even though it may go against "the system" or inherited blueprint. There is a reason you can't get it out of your head and heart. The persistent presence of your dreams in your thoughts and heart signifies a higher calling, a beckoning from the depths of your soul.

What are you truly being called to do?

Who are you being called to be?

What is your desired impact?

LIFE REVIEW

Look back on your life right now like today is your last day on Earth and answer the following questions:

- Did you live as the person you were born to be, or did you live life as a character in someone else's story?
- What would you have done differently?
- What risks or opportunities would you take?
- What impact would you have liked to have on others and the world around you?

The matters of life and death are all connected. Once you understand that you came into this world for a unique reason, tailored precisely to who you are, you can start living a deliberate and purpose-driven life.

You can find the Life Review worksheet in your resource kit.

Chapter 8:

THE DECEPTION OF HAPPILY EVER AFTER

"Never underestimate the power you have to take your life in a new direction."

— *Germany Kent*

AND THEY LIVED HAPPILY EVER AFTER...

This is how most fairy tales and childhood stories end.. They always lived happily ever after. Even at the end of movies, the characters that we were so invested in for two hours rode off into the sunset into their seemingly perfect lives. If you look closely, we were subliminally forced to believe this narrative in multiple areas. In education, we are told that if we get that degree, then we will make a lot of money and have a good life. In some religions we were told, if we pass the test of going through extreme struggles and trials, we would receive a great reward at the end, not realizing some of those struggles were self-inflicted. We were told that if we followed a certain way of life, went through certain experiences, or if we followed a specific path, we were guaranteed to "live happily ever after."

This is extremely inaccurate.

In the happily ever after, you have reached the ultimate level where there are no worries, life is good and without trial or struggle. You have beaten all the levels in the game of life, and now you are problem-free. This is not real. This does not exist. Unfortunately, no matter how much education or critical thinking skills we have, some of us are committed to this narrative, which is a dangerous place to live. The happily ever after can cause us to make decisions that lead us down the wrong path, decisions that take us away from our mission, and decisions that give us a false hope of security and success. These decisions can drastically change the trajectory of our lives. Especially those of us who grew up in the purity culture, where we were told that if we waited to have sex until after marriage, we would have this magical life and an unbreakable relationship. Unfortunately, so many of us fell into this trap.

Growing up, I saw so many people get married young and unprepared, thinking that if they got married, all their problems would go away. I was one of them. Marriage was the epitome of success. I thought if I was married, my happily ever after would begin. If I please God and do all the things that are expected of me, then all the blessings would flow, and I wouldn't have to worry about anything anymore. I almost laugh at this sentiment now. We have had generations of people believe these lies and some still believe these lies. It is tragic.

The deception of happily ever after applies to so many things in life. It causes us to believe that everything will be perfect once we have the "thing," whatever that may be. It causes us to think that we will be absolved from any responsibility and leads us to believe that there will be a time when all our problems will cease. It causes us to hold our breath and not enjoy life even through trials. We grind and work so hard to get the relationship, get the job, make the move, reach the goal, and once we have it, problems are still there, and we are baffled! How dare I still have problems now that I'm married! I make six figures; why am I still struggling with this?!

Another tragedy in the happily ever after is that we decide that we will start living once we achieve that goal. We tell ourselves that we will be happy when…, we will slow down when…, we will be complete when… we will live then… We go through life numb, avoiding experiences, avoiding lessons, and don't truly live because we think life starts after we achieve our goals. Even after you have dismantled the system, destroyed your mask, and achieved your goals, there will still be obstacles and trials you will have to face. When times get tough, it is easy to resort back to old ways. You must develop tools and skills to stay the course and not revert to old habits such as negative self-talk and other unhealthy habits.

I have an issue with negative self-talk. Whenever I mess up, feel ugly, experience rejection, etc., I sometimes resort to talking down to myself. However, I have learned to affirm my way through the struggle. I repeat affirmations of hope. Affirmations like:

- *I am capable of doing difficult things.*
- *I am loved and worthy to receive love.*
- *I am financially abundant and can afford to pay my bills.*
- *I am powerful, strong, and supported every step of the way.*
- *No matter the circumstance, anything that is for me is mine.*

Affirmations are more than just words. Affirmations can help change our reality. The way we speak to ourselves matters.

According to Dr. Andrew Newberg, "A single word has the power to influence the expression of genes that regulate physical and emotional stress$_6$." When you hold optimistic words in your mind, it activates your frontal lobe. This part of the brain is linked to language and movement and is responsible for moving you into action. Research shows that the more you concentrate on positive words, the more it affects other areas of your brain$_6$. Thoughts become words, and words become actions. Allow the positive affirmations to get into your brain and heart because if you believe, you can have the ability to change your reality.

As you are navigating on the journey less traveled and encountering new things, you must develop practices that will help you deal with issues and circumstances that may arise along the way. Remember, this journey is a lot like walking the tightrope I mentioned in Chapter 3. To stay steady and anchored, you must have enough faith to take the step right in front of you while keeping your focus on the divine – the Ultimate Compass.

Here are some of the practices you can develop to support you in your journey:

- Meditation: Develop a consistent mediation practice. Make time each day that is dedicated to meditation. For example, I include a 10-20-minute meditation session in my morning routine. You may do something different. Make sure it is a time when you will not be interrupted. My child knows that when it is time to meditate, she is not to interrupt. You may miss a day here and there, but if you are consistent, meditation will become a natural part of your life.

- Prayer: This can be a part of your meditation practice or a separate thing. I suggest doing this daily and often.

- Journaling: Have a journal to record your thoughts, feelings, ideas, and messages.

- Affirmations: Write them out and place them where you can see them. As soon as you have a negative thought, cancel and combat that thought with a positive affirmation. It may be helpful to say specific affirmations in the morning and throughout the day. You can find a list of affirmations in your resource kit.

- Reflection: Take time to reflect on what you have learned about yourself and others. Also, reflect on the experiences you have had, how you may want to do things differently, or what you would like to experience in the future.

- Give yourself permission to pivot and evolve. As you have new experiences and learn new things, you may find that you no longer want to do something or that you want to change directions. That is ok. Give yourself permission to change the course. Life is all about the journey and lessons learned.

- Give yourself grace: You will mess up, and things will not work out all the time. Some of the systems we were raised in did not allow us to make mistakes without receiving damnation. No one is perfect. Get up, dust yourself off, and try again.

- Rest: This journey can be emotional and overwhelming. Take deliberate pauses to replenish your energy and give yourself the space needed for healing and rejuvenation. In honoring your need for rest, you nurture your inner resilience and create a solid foundation from which to continue your path of self-discovery, growth, and transformation.

Chapter 9:

DIE EMPTY

"The richest place on earth is the cemetery because that's where you'll find all the hopes and dreams that were never fulfilled, the books that were never written, the songs that were never sung, the inventions that were never shared, the cures that were never discovered, all because someone was too afraid to take that first step, keep with the problem, or determined to carry out their dream."

— *Les Brown*

A s a death doula, I have chosen to work in the pre-death role of helping people do legacy work and making end-of-life preparations. At times, I sit with those who are actively dying to provide comfort and support. One of the phrases I have heard often from the dying or their families regarding the end of their life is, "I wish I had…", "I should have.", "I would have…". People often get to the end and look back and see the things they would have done differently or identify things they were supposed to do but did not. They lived all their lives thinking they had to be a certain way or do certain things, only to realize that they either wasted time doing things that didn't serve them or never had the chance to do something they have always dreamed of. We will all pass away eventually. We often take advantage of the time we have and think we will get to it later, but later never comes. If you want or feel led to do something, take the inspired action and do it now. If your "system" is keeping you back from your greatness, dismantle it. If those generational traditions and curses are holding you back, break them. If your mind has been brainwashed to think that you are less than or incapable, fight against that narrative. I encourage you to do everything you can to die empty. Die knowing you came to Earth to do what you were supposed to do, be who you were created to be, and leave nothing behind that you wished you had done or accomplished.

Whether it be dismantling systems of oppression, going against the things you were originally taught, decolonizing your mind, or just living according to who you really are, it can be an extremely scary journey. You are traveling down a road you have never traveled before. I must warn you that this journey is not all sunshine and rainbows. There will be times when you want to give up because it is hard, and you won't have a playbook to follow. However, you are equipped with the power and the strength to succeed. In my upbringing as a Christian, I learned the importance of prayer and seeking divine guidance in all aspects of life. However, this sometimes led to the misconception that prayer alone would relieve me of personal responsibility. When my prayers didn't bring immediate results and situations became worse, I felt helpless, attributing it to punishment or the consequences of my actions. This mindset is profoundly misleading and can be dangerous. It's crucial to recognize that you possess the ability and strength to achieve remarkable things, even through struggle.

Is God not powerful? If we were created in the image of God, aren't we powerful too?

During this journey, I fully realized my power and the responsibility I had to change my reality. I also realized that in some areas, I allowed myself to be a victim and chose to stay in certain situations instead of accessing the power in me to make a change. We all have this power. We all can change our reality and have the life we desire. Life isn't fair, and there are times when we cannot change the situation alone, but we can change the way we look at and deal with the situation. Through prayer, meditation, and working on the shadows of your inner self, you can access the power that has always resided in you.

YOU ARE powerful.

YOU ARE beautiful.

YOU ARE worthy.

YOU ARE successful.

YOU ARE enough.

YOU CAN do hard things.

YOU CAN live a life of freedom and purpose.

Why?

Because you are made from POWER.

Power runs through your veins. No matter the trial or the situation, you have the tools to make it through and are supported the entire time. Once you understand this, you will be able to take life head-on, receive the blessings that are meant for you, and do all the things that you are supposed to do and more. Tap into your power and do the work. Life can be beautiful if you recognize and use what is already within. Stay on that tightrope, walk in faith, and when times get hard, and it is hard to see the journey in front of you, stand in your power and be who you were created to be!

Destroy the Mask!

EPILOGUE

Now that you have reached the end of the book, you have the tools it takes to begin the journey of removing the mask, start taking actionable steps to live out your purpose, and start the foundation of leaving a legacy of power. Don't read this book and continue living life wearing your mask. Use this book as a catalyst to catapult you into the life you desire and achieve the things you dream about.

The following summary highlights the journey I took you through in this book.

Chapter 1: Taking Inventory: Take inventory of the things that have caused you to wear a mask.

Chapter 2: Addressing the Baggage: Identify and address the baggage and limiting beliefs you have picked up along the way.

Chapter 3: The Tightrope Experience: Understand that for you to take this journey, you must have the courage to be divinely guided.

Chapter 4: Listen to your Intuition: Developing and listening to your intuition will help you navigate through fear and uncertainty.

Chapter 5: Turning Dreams into Reality: Get your dreams out of your head and turn them into goals.

Chapter 6: The Truth about Manifestation: Manifestation is not a magic trick. Manifestation requires work on our part.

Chapter 7: Determine your Impact: Our dreams are connected to our purpose. Our purpose is not for us and should be used to impact others around us and those who come after us.

Chapter 8: The Deception of Happily Ever After: Even after we achieve our goals and get where we want to be, there will still be obstacles. You have the tools and the ability to overcome issues you encounter along the way.

Chapter 9: Die Empty: To die empty is knowing you came here to do what you were supposed to do. You have the power and responsibility to change your reality.

ABOUT THE AUTHOR

ERIN FAITH KABBA is an educator and Rebirth-to-Death Doula who has a passion for life and legacy. After destroying her mask, created by harmful religious indoctrination, societal norms, and limiting beliefs, Erin went through her rebirth. She realized that she was living out of alignment with who she really was and what she was purposed to do. Once she started the journey of destroying her mask, there was no looking back. She made the commitment that she would always strive to live life in alignment with her authentic self, even if it went against the norm. After prayer, research, deep meditation, and doing the work, she was able to transform areas of her life and achieve things she never thought were possible! She realized that life is precious and wants to depart this earth leaving a legacy while knowing she did exactly what she came here to do. She is devoted to helping women achieve the same.

Erin is the owner of The Oya Collective, LLC, where she supports women in having transformational rebirths, empowers them to live with audacity, and helps them take steps to leave an impactful legacy. She has 15+ years of experience as an educator in K-12, university, and corporate settings. She lives outside of Washington D.C. with her family.

RESOURCE KIT

Complete the following activities in the journal pages at the end
of the kit, in your own journal, or using the digital resource kit at
www.theoyacollective.com/resources

CHAPTER 1: TAKE INVENTORY

Reflection Questions

1. What blueprint were you taught to follow?

2. What factors contributed to forming your identity?

3. Are there cracks in your foundation? If so, in what areas?

4. Has something ever prompted you to take inventory of your beliefs? If so, what?

INVENTORY PROCESS WORKSHEET

Believe/Resonates	Do Not Believe/Does Not Resonate	Unsure

CHAPTER 2: ADDRESSING THE BAGGAGE

The following page contains reflection questions and journal prompts for you to identify and address your limiting beliefs. You may use the reflection questions as a journal prompt or they can be used to guide your thinking for the journal prompts.

REFLECTION QUESTIONS AND JOURNAL PROMPTS

Reflection Question 1:

What beliefs about yourself have stopped you from pursuing dreams or opportunities?

_____

_____

_____

_____

_____

Journal Prompt 1:

Reflect on specific areas in your life where your limiting beliefs have impacted your decisions. What did those beliefs tell you? How did they change your decisions?

_____

_____

_____

_____

_____

Reflection Question 2:
Do your limiting beliefs stem from external factors such as family beliefs or societal norms, or do they stem from your own experiences or perceptions?

_____

_____

_____

_____

Journal Prompt 2:
List out your limiting beliefs or negative beliefs you may have about yourself or your ability. Then, identify what experience or person led you to have that belief. Lastly, write a counterargument or positive statement that challenges the accuracy of that belief.

_____

_____

_____

_____

Reflection Question 3:
How would letting go of these limiting beliefs impact your self-confidence, self-esteem, or outlook on life?

_____

_____

_____

_____

Journal Prompt 3: Imagine a life where you no longer have the limiting beliefs you have been holding on to. What would that life look like? How would you feel? Visualize it and be detailed!

CHAPTER 3: THE TIGHTROPE EXPERIENCE

Identifying Core Values

Step 1: Answer the following questions.

Based on what you have learned about yourself and what resonates with you, how do you want to show up in the world?

What values or virtues do you now prioritize or want to prioritize in your relationships, work, and personal life?

What values would best support your well-being, self-care, and overall mental, emotional, and physical health?

What are some signs or feelings that something is in alignment with your true self?

Which fundamental principles and values from your upbringing would you like to preserve and carry forward in your journey?

_____

_____

_____

_____

LIST OF CORE VALUES

Authenticity	Faith	Leadership	Respect
Balance	Fame	Liberation	Responsibility
Beauty	Friendships	Love	Security
Boldness	Fun	Loyalty	Self-Respect
Compassion	Growth	Meaningful Work	Service
Challenge	Happiness	Openness	Spirituality
Citizenship	Honesty	Optimism	Stability
Community	Humor	Peace	Success
Contribution	Influence	Pleasure	Trustworthiness
Creativity	Inner Harmony	Poise	Wealth
Curiosity	Justice	Popularity	Wisdom
Determination	Kindness	Religion	
Fairness	Knowledge	Reputation	

Adapted from James Clear

Step 2: Identify your Top 3 Core Values

These core values will serve as an anchor as you proceed on your journey. They will serve as a compass to help guide choices and actions. Please choose core values from the list above or values that are not on the list. Write them down or highlight them on the list.

CORE VALUES

CHAPTER 5: TURNING DREAMS INTO REALITY

In the space below, identify everything that you would like to accomplish or receive. If you feel like you are being led to do or explore something, but it isn't extremely clear, write that down as well. Be as detailed as possible.

CHAPTER 6: THE TRUTH ABOUT MANIFESTATION

Prepare for the Manifestation

Choose 3 goals/dreams from the previous activity and identify everything that is in your power to do to be prepared to receive that manifestation or accomplish the goal.

Dream:1

Dream:2

Dream:3

CHAPTER 7: DETERMINE YOUR IMPACT

Life Review Worksheet

Look back on your life right now like today is your last day on Earth and answer the following questions:

- Did you live as the person you were born to be, or did you live life as a character in someone else's story?

_____

_____

_____

_____

- What would you have done differently?

_____

_____

_____

- What risks or opportunities would you take?

_____

_____

_____

_____

- What impact would you have liked to have on others and the world around you?

_____

_____

_____

_____

CHAPTER 8: THE DECEPTION OF HAPPILY EVER AFTER
Affirmation List

The following list contains affirmations for you to use to combat negative thoughts. They aim to help push you through difficult times. Say them, embody them, believe them.

• *I am capable of doing difficult things.*	• *I am powerful, beautiful, and successful.*
• *I am loved and am worthy to receive love.*	• *I allow myself to slow down and enjoy the present.*
• *I am financially abundant.*	• *I can be happy while experiencing struggle.*
• *I am powerful, strong, and supported every step of the way.*	• *Today, I only worry about things that I can control.*
• *In every situation, I choose peace.*	• *Today, I give myself grace.*
• *Even when the world around me is chaotic, I remain powerful and strong.*	• *I allow myself to evolve.*
• *I deserve good things.*	• *I recognize that criticism often reflects other people's perspectives and not my true worth.*
• *I am at peace with where I am at right now.*	• *I am worthy of love and respect regardless of others' opinions.*
• *My journey is MY journey, their journey is THEIR journey.*	• *I embrace my uniqueness and authenticity.*
• *What is for me will not bypass me.*	
• *I am in control of my feelings and reactions.*	

JOURNAL PAGES

Use the following pages to write down thoughts or things that came up in your reading or reflection.

SOURCE LIST

Keiling, H. (2023, July 31). *Core Values in the Workplace: 84 Powerful Examples*. Core Values in the Workplace: 84 Powerful Examples. Retrieved September 29, 2023, from **https://www.indeed. com/career-advice/career-development/core-values**

Cambridge University Press (n.d.). *Intuition*. Cambridge Dictionary. Retrieved September 29, 2023, from **https://dictionary. cambridge.org/dictionary/english/intuition**

Lloyd, O. (2019, September 13). *What Really is the Ego? And How Do We Control it?* Medium. Retrieved September 29, 2023, from **https://medium.com/swlh/what-really-is-the-ego-and-how-do-we-control-it-9de0bbe87110#:~: text=The%20ego%20is%20 simply%20our, or%20inferior%20to%20other%20people**

Rankin, L. (2023, April 12). *18 Ways To Develop & Strengthen Your Intuition*. Mindbodygreeen. Retrieved September 29, 2023, from **https://www.mindbodygreen.com/articles/how-to-strengthen-your-intuition**

(2015, June 3). *Changing the Face of Medicine*. National Institutes of Health. Retrieved September 29, 2023, from **https://cfmedi-cine.nlm.nih.gov/physicians/biography_73.html**

Horton, L. (2019, August 8). *The Neuroscience Behind Our Words*. BRM Institute. Retrieved September 29, 2023, from **https://brm. institute/neuroscience-behind-words/**

Clear, J. (n.d.). *Core Values List*. James Clear. Retrieved September 29, 2023, from **https://jamesclear.com/core-values**

www.ingramcontent.com/pod-product-compliance
Lightning Source LLC
Chambersburg PA
CBHW070439130626
46553CB00006B/2251